CREATIVE IN GOD'S IMAGE
Engaging the Creative Good

Copyright © 2014 Nate Pruitt.
All rights reserved.

Except for brief quotations in reviews, no part of this book may be reproduced without prior written permission from the publisher.

www.natepruitt.com

ISBN 13: 978-0-9915491-1-5

Cover design courtesy of Ryan Tempro.

Dedicated to Dave Gajda,

Whose conversations were the first sparks of this book.
And whose questions continue to make me dig deeper.

Contents

Acknowledgements

Introduction

Chapter 1 Creative Obedience

Chapter 2 Get Ready to Dance

Chapter 3 When a Dance Partner Falls

Chapter 4 Realigning the Dream

Chapter 5 Repentance and the Life After

Chapter 6 Humility Trumps Self Esteem

Chapter 7 Speaking in Faith

Chapter 8 Running in Faith

Chapter 9 Worship is a Many Splendored Thing

Chapter 10 Shameless Worship

Author Information

Acknowledgements

First I would like to thank and acknowledge Dave Gajda, to whom this book is dedicated, because he went with me into more conversations about creativity than anyone else at a time when I needed the reminder the most. While I thought I was helping him what was really happening was a spark was beginning to burn deep within me, and once those flames were fanned this book began to form.

I also owe more thanks than I can adequately express to Amy Lutes. Not only has she provided me with insightful and encouraging editing, but she's been my partner in crime for years as a fellow writer. Completing my own book excites me almost as much as the coming completion of many incredible novels and other works from her. She has understood my struggles as a writer in ways that others could not, but hasn't allowed me to remain mired down in those frustrations. I am continually indebted to her as a friend and peer and can't see any way I could possible repay all of her kindness and support. Likewise, I must thank her husband, Brien, for pushing me in his own way and for letting me occupy far too much of her time with my frustrations and editing needs.

In addition I need to thank Ryan Tempro for

getting onboard quickly and turning a concept in my head into a design for the cover. His professionalism and enthusiasm are inspiring. I should also thank my pastor, Phil Lindsley, for seeing the spark in me and reminding me to push on toward the continually calling voice of God. He is a mentor and dear friend that insists on checking in on me when I don't even realize how deep my need may be.

There are many others that I won't be able to list here because of the vast quantity of conversations and interactions that have helped form this work. Likewise, there have been too many to count who have offered an encouraging word at just the right time. I could fill pages with those who fall under this category and still come up short.

I need to thank my parents for continually believing that I could do such things. All too often I hear of parents pushing their children toward their own concept of success, while mine have continually insisted that I obey God and live the life set before me. They have taught me more than I will ever know, but each day I catch a new glimpse of seeds that have set deep roots. And finally, I am ever grateful for my wife, Sabrina, who pushed me as a writer by being the biggest fan of my writing, and also my beautiful children, who remind me every day that they love me relentlessly and that I am also called to love them deeply—a calling I love to seek and obey.

Introduction

This book is the result of hundreds of conversations causing my mind to reel with possibilities. Many of those conversations were with my buddy Dave. When Dave and I first started talking a few years back the discussions varied over a wide range of subjects, and they still do to this day, but it feels like they have centered on one theme. He wanted to build, to create, to make things of worth, and I realized that was exactly what I wanted, too. Whether it was to entertain, educate, enhance something that was already present, or to do something completely strange and new, the desire was to create.

It's natural to have a discussion from one place sit in your mind and then see those themes spill over into other aspects of your life. Before long I realized that I was having very similar conversations with a large number of people. It seemed that we all desired to participate in life in such a way that we were creating, and as those conversations deepened it became clear that we all want to create something for *good*.

Creation isn't a wasted act. Not only does creating make a difference in the lives of those who experience the results, it also impacts and forms the one creating in a significant way. We are all, in some form or another (but really in multiple ways), called to creating. It's hardwired in us. However, since it looks completely unique in each of us there are many who feel they don't have a purpose of creating. Perhaps that is due to an overemphasis of creativity *only* being linked to a few forms of art. But that couldn't be further from the truth.

Whenever we engage the world, it comes with a level of creativity. Creativity comes in many forms. Whether you're a songwriter pouring your heart out into lyrics, an analyst who is vigorously seeking a statistical link in cause and effect, the author of a moving novel, or the attorney drafting a binding contract that will protect your client, you are creating. We all engage the world with creativity, and if we do it well, we also enhance the world by doing so.

When I returned to school to complete my degree in youth ministry, I spent a prolonged time in my Biblical Hebrew class examining the first chapter of Genesis. I was captured by this God who not only creates, but who created us in the image and likeness of God. We are destined to be creators. I so wanted to walk in the apprenticeship of being a creator learning from God. The journey has been difficult, but the lessons I continue to learn are life changing. It is my deep hope and prayer that in reading this simple book there will be inspiration and clarity that may help change your life, too.

This book has been written in a straight forward fashion with the hope that the reader can engage with it quickly and thoroughly without being drawn out of the creative flow. Fear attempts to disrupt us as much as it seeks to dissuade us. From that fear, we find procrastination via distractions as a salve, when really it's a source of further pain. To that end, it is my hope that this book will provide concise encouragement so that you can get back to the tasks that define living for God's creative good in your life.

Grace and peace,

Nate Pruitt

Chapter One
Creative Obedience

Creativity in God is a wide open world. Think of it as a garden so full of freedom, nourishment, and blessing that almost all of the space of life is an example of absolute joy. The truth is that we are called into this sort of creative space. Worship is life, and we are called to live our lives before God with great freedom and joyful praise.

This book is designed to encourage the pursuit of knowing and living this freedom. I can guarantee that I don't have a perfect formula to free your creativity. Not only that, but every book I have read on the subject—and there have been a lot, most of which I rather enjoyed—included some sort of formula. More importantly, while most of these books were Christian-themed, the formula ended up being a series of things for the reader to do independently while God was only mentioned occasionally.

I can't write one of those books. I can't write a formula. Here is why: with every formula and system that I have read there has come a moment in my own life when God has stopped me in my tracks and broken me free of those formulaic guidelines so I could walk in the freedom of the Divine presence as a creative being made in the image and likeness of the Creator.

One book told me I shouldn't quit my job until my creative passion was financially paving the way for me to make that transition responsibly. I really liked that book, and that advice made a ton of sense to me—especially since I had already made the mistake of quitting a job without a financial safety net once (which I'll elaborate on soon). However, as I type this I am in a season in which God led me to step away from my paying job to pursue the creative ministry I was called to do. While I'm smiling now, I can tell you I didn't find it that funny at the time. Still, when God puts a call on our lives it includes a journey that comes complete with our Heavenly Guide and godly provision.

To see the things of God, we have to see past our reality into the potential of what a life lived in God can bear. We also have to see past limitations, and that includes the limiting of our creativity to one aspect. As Robert A. Heinlein put it in *Time Enough for Love* (1973), "Specialization is for insects." I can't write a book about how God wants to use your singular specific gift for the work of the Kingdom of Heaven, because God has made you an elaborate creative being with nuanced and varied gifts and graces.

Focusing on one gift misses the point that worship is about a whole life lived for God. Imagination will allow us to understand that God can improve upon and bless all aspects of our lives. It would be ridiculous for me to attempt to write the formula for how this is to be done. The sheer complexity of it would require endless writing and knowledge that extends well beyond my capacity. Rather, it can only be found in the space of endless prayer. In this way there is the freedom to imagine and create in and with God. Rather than providing a formula, my hope for this work is to remind us all of truths that we often overlook and to enable us to see them—and God—with greater freedom and imagination so that our creative nature can thrive.

Creative interpretation

The best thing I was ever taught while studying theology in college was that if you can't read the Bible with imagination then you can't see what God is saying. I've found that to be quite true, especially coupled with something equally profound I was taught outside of school: sometimes the most obvious things in the Bible are the things we overlook.

Think about those two statements for a minute and I'm sure you'll begin to couple the thoughts, but I'm willing to save you the time. I've noticed that when I miss the things that are most obvious in scripture, it is because I've stopped reading the Word with an actively imaginative openness to God.

One example of what I'm talking about is something my dad pointed out to me in a conversation about faith when he alluded to Matthew 18:1-4 and pointed out that, while we can greatly expound upon what faith like a child looks like, we are foolish to overlook what it quite literally looked like to those gathered on that day: Jesus called the child and the child came to him. Do you see it? The simple and yet profound nature of what just happened?

As a pastor I know that it is easy enough to fly right past this leaving it unaddressed as an outline develops about characteristics of children. Pretty soon we're talking about how children have needs, citing other scriptures about God providing in the nature of the Heavenly Father and more. While these are excellent points, it behooves us to not overlook the fact that *Jesus called the child* and *the child came to him*. That is quite the visual example of faith that teaches that when Jesus calls there is, and should be, unhesitating and unquestioning obedience. Thus faith in action is a monster of a sermon.

Even before that conversation with my dad, I had run into another instance of something very obvious and right in front of us being overlooked in another passage. When I first heard it taught I had left out my imagination and an openness to the Spirit to speak directly within the text. The matter came about when rereading the first chapter of Genesis. In the creation account provided right there is a statement made about man and woman, that they (we, humankind) were created in the likeness and image of God.

The interesting thing is that any time I'd confronted that passage in commentaries, expositions, sermons, or any other context there was an immediate jump to find out what the image of God was and—*whoosh!*—we were whisked away from that chapter and passage to some other place in scripture that described God. The things I heard were beautiful and inspiring, such as God is love and we are made with the need of love and the capacity for love, and this is a significant reality (and necessary to teach).

However, we'd ceased to talk about the Creator as creative, and we'd run away from acknowledging that one of the first things that is true of us is that we are called to lives painted with an expressive nature of creating in and for God.

Obedience is a creative calling when it comes to the life of one who accepts Christ as Lord. Faith in God is an immediate invitation to a creative lifestyle, because the world's sense of "normal" has little to nothing to do with an obedient lifestyle before God. Rather than risk for the Kingdom we prefer to maintain the *status quo* and find our joy in God lacking as a result. Such unnatural living is always unsatisfying.

My hope and passionate desire for this book is that it will push you forward, not through formulation, but by reminding you that the God who *calls* us continues to be the voice which *guides* us across dry land where a sea once stood, through the wilderness, and into a Promised Land. The manner in which such things occur is nothing short of creative and inspired.

A personal reflection
A few years ago I knew God was calling me into a season of writing. I prayed about it with an extreme tenacity. I had a job at the time, and though it wasn't paying much it paid better than nothing. I also had recently married, which was

a great blessing, and I knew that she loved me so I didn't want to do anything crazy to mess things up.

For a torturous duration I wrestled with what was clearly the will of God. The message to make a big change came up over and over again on the radio, in sermons at our church, in every book I read (and I started trying to escape it and those books still got me)—even in casual conversations. Finally I accepted that God was leading me, tendered my resignation and stepped forward into a dangerous new world.

At this point in the story it would be great to have a series of miracles to tell you about how God provided. There were many, but the truth is that they quickly dried up because I grew disobedient almost immediately. I was called to write, but the funny thing about being called by God to do something is that it will require faith in action. Things started to get hard. Obeying God wasn't without its challenges, fears and frustrations. I became consumed with these things rather than with God and writing.

Things began to fall apart. I picked up another job that was nothing close to what I was supposed to be doing. The job was just a microcosm of my general frustration with life. We weren't making enough to stay where we were staying, which was unfortunate since I happened to be enrolled in college pursuing a degree for my call as a minister, yet that was another thing we couldn't afford.

Finally it all crashed down. I had given up on my calling and the Caller. I was AWOL, a deserter, and utterly miserable. Unemployment, class failures, eviction and depression all became a part of my life at that time. Really they had become a part of *our* lives at that time. I thought I wanted the adventure but thought it was something to do on my own.

The sin of rebellion cost my family greatly. By the time everything had fallen apart we even had a baby girl. Knowing how dangerous my sin had become for my family almost destroyed me. We moved in with my in-laws. I began to wander in a spiritual wilderness.

Moses and Egypt
Moses' story in the Bible is incredible. I don't know when he first began to understand that it was about time that the Egyptians were no longer given rein to oppress the Hebrew people, but I can assure you there was strong conviction long before he saw any enflamed bushes.

The story of Moses as murderer is a big insight

into the fact that he was only partially grasping the truth God wanted to show him. By his own hands he tried to find a way to be an answer to the problem. That's the dangerous form of creativity, not to mention the disobedient kind. Such disobedience is part and parcel with the mindset that calls on God only when things are out of hand rather than always seeking God as Lord and Guide.

Moses' disobedience was similar to my own in that God had big plans, but we had dumb ideas and the will to rush ahead and act them out in proud sinfulness.

Creativity is only a blessing when done within the freedom of obeying God.

Often we lose sight of what creativity really is because we think that it is synonymous with independence, but being creative apart from the will of God is the wrong sort of risk. There is a great cost with such actions. There are both immediate consequences, and long standing ones, if we don't repent. These consequences are never just ours to bear, either. There are always more casualties than we realize.

I know that I hurt my wife and daughter by my disobedience, even though my little girl was too small to realize it at the time. When Moses reflected on how God used him to lead he began to understand that he had hurt his people by initially trying to lead his own way.

Disobedience comes with great cost, obedience comes with great blessing. Creativity is at its fullest when we grasp that an immense Creator who is well beyond our mental capacities is calling us to participate in the ongoing (re)creation of the world.

Chapter Two
Get Ready to Dance

There is a poignant beauty to the *triquetra*, the image used to represent the Trinity. With three points representing—in no particular order—Father, Son, and Spirit, it would have been easy enough to make it a triangle. But the image is deeper than that as each line crosses the other two so that while all corners are connected to each other they don't simply *get* connected, they *dance* there.

Within the image you can see the beauty of many old forms of dance that used to occur when communities would gather to celebrate. Rather than couples dancing the night away, or individuals trying to find another body to grind against, everyone gathered to be caught up in a spinning, twisting, and flowing procession that would fill a room with one synchronized movement. To dance was to make all gathered participate as one, so that each part functioned as a complement to the whole.

I remember a little something of this from my childhood in school when we would be gathered into the gym for physical education and, to the great sorrow of all involved, would be stuck with square dancing rather than some form of sport. Square dancing was the scourge of physical education classes, and since it usually lasted a week or two we were all pretty sure we were coming down with something as soon as that part of the school year began.

Despite our griping and the fact that we generally had very little say in choosing either our partners or the larger groups of eight individuals per square, something peculiar would always happen as the days went on. A strange phenomenon would come over us to where we actually wanted to do things well. The individuals who wanted to persist in making a mockery of the whole thing would be called out by their groups to allow everyone to have a better time by moving the way we were supposed to, and if you looked close enough you could even catch everyone smiling on occasion with a sense of accomplishment and togetherness.

We are invited into a similar type of dance that resembles the dance of the Trinity, the three parts of God that are each fully God and complementary of the others. The invitation for all who are created in God's likeness and imagery—which we're first shown in Genesis chapter one means all of humankind—is to keep participating in the dance. The dance was started with the dawn of creation, and although the universe has continued to participate we humans have often struggled to engage.

Perhaps this is why all creation groans (see Romans 8:19-22), because it is *humanity* that fails to participate in the dance properly, like a foolish school ager acting out of immature rebellion. The invitation is for humanity to embrace the creativity with which we were made that we may participate in this dance in the same manner as God dances harmoniously within the Trinity.

Welcome to the dance
The invitation into the dance with God is a very intimate one. In that moment when we draw into our call as we understand it often comes at a period of spiritual clarity and closeness to God. While the moment doesn't require a worship service, it does require an acute awareness of God's presence and voice.

Case in point: I knew a guy who one day regained consciousness after a party full of drugs and alcohol and reached under the chair he had passed out on, trying to find a bottle that wasn't completely empty. However, what his hand hit was a Bible. As he looked around his living room and saw the many bodies strewn all over the floor and furniture from the hard partying the night before he was open to hear

God. He got his wife up, they went to church that morning and by the end of the service gave their lives over to God.

This true story is pretty extreme, your situation may be more traditional, but at some point in time, if you are pursuing what you would refer to as a calling, there was a closeness and openness to God that enabled you to be aware of the fact you are called.

Time to go for a walk
God is a meandering wanderer. Think of it this way: God isn't worried about the boundaries of what we perceive to be the dance floor. God is active presence, not a mythical old king with a huge beard sitting at a distance unmoved. God loves to be the action that leads to where the action is. This was true of God in the Garden of Eden, it was true of God leading up to and after the exodus from Egypt, and when inhabiting the Promised Land didn't sound good enough, God was up for a wilderness hike first.

Christ wandered with the same spirit of the Father. Even though it would have seemed logical for the ministry of Christ to have been centered (and maybe exclusively located) in Jerusalem, he treated Jerusalem as a place to visit, not reside. Christ wandered rebelliously, as perceived by the culture of that day, even wandering into land reserved for the Samaritans, the most detestable members of humanity, whom He visited numerous times.

God preferred a tabernacle, a place of worship that was also portable, back when other gods had temples. Wanting to keep up with other cultures Israel desired a temple and God allowed one to be built, but then let the chosen people know that it was not the sole dwelling place of the Holy presence, but rather a footstool.

God refuses to be boxed in. God seeks to be on the move. The Holy Spirit is even directly compared to wind and breath, a constant fluctuation and movement. God is ever moving, creatively and harmoniously. We are invited to this dance.

"So what?" you may ask. Well the question then is: *Are you moving with God*? If God is a constant mover are you open to this movement? We tend to want to hunker down and build up walls—let's get settled, let's get secure, let's get familiar with a small area, virtually immobilize ourselves and call it a day (or a life).

Our culture teaches us to do everything we can for a stagnant lifestyle. Words like "steady income" and "job security" become our greatest motivators. We see provision as the result of man's great willingness to be a real stick in the mud. The deeper you sink in the better off you are come a storm, right? But such devices are like sand, an easily blown away false sense of security.

Ever notice that the preferred structure type of God was one built on a rock, not one built with a deep footer and elaborate foundation connected to nothing? Guess what—that stick in the mud is a house built on sand that will quickly erode away well beyond your ability or control. God loves movement, and God is steady. We fear movement, and try to anchor in that which we think is stable, but is easily moved. Why? Because we're still not so sure we can trust God.

In *The Lion, The Witch, & The Wardrobe* the question is asked of Aslan, "Then he isn't safe?" To which the reply is, "'Course he's not safe. But he's good. He's the King, I tell you." We want a safe God, a God who does as we ask, asks little to nothing of us in return, and shows sappy goodness and kindness to us so we can live lives of ease and comfort. No such deal will be struck for it is antithetical to scripture.

If we really want to get down to it those most beloved of Christ, such as John and Peter, were far from having the cushiest lives. Threats, torture, imprisonment, and even martyrdom (or a life sentence in John's case) were all a part of their earthly existence. Yet, when God moved- they moved. That movement with God is what righteousness is, and what faithfulness looks like.

When believing isn't enough

What does this have to do with all of us as we understand we are called by God? Well, it means we are called into a journey that is more than a mental exercise in the belief of the existence of God. James points out that even the demons believe in God, and they shudder. But it can become too easy for us to simply believe in God and shrug that off as a mental area that is compartmentalized and separate from the structured aspects of our daily lives.

Basically, we *say* we believe in God, but we don't bother getting close enough to God to allow ourselves to *trust* God. God is very easy to "believe in" when all that belief requires of us is to admit that God exists. That's culturally acceptable in our society, so nothing more is required of us and no trust is necessary. God can be real because we accept God to be real in our minds—a concept usually reserved for Santa and the fairies of Peter Pan's Neverland.

Trusting God is hard because we only want to do so part way. We will trust in God to get started on something but, like impatient and stubborn children, we will try to rush ahead without further instructions. Don't believe me? Just try to explain an organized game to kids once you've already put them in position and given them the equipment. It just doesn't make sense because they are overwhelmed with the desire to already be playing.

We often want to run headlong into what we "know" we're supposed to do (pride) because we want to put ourselves in the best position for ease (out of fear, which is pride unmasked) because we're scared God will put us somewhere in which we are uncertain we can succeed (mistrust). God, however, is all about on-the-job training. He puts us where He wants us knowing that for us to succeed we have to keep listening for further instructions. Sadly, we often don't.

Instead of listening to God, we get so sucked into the *doing* that we exert all of our energy on that part of the process. Then we start failing because we're trying to do on our own what can only be done with God. Next thing we know we're trying to emotionally rationalize the failing and we're grieving. Finally, still isolated on our own accord, we get frustrated with God.

And God is wondering why we stopped drawing close to Him and listening.

Accusing God is self-indictment

The story of the fall of man told in Genesis is an incredible one. God is, as we've mentioned, this amazing meandering wanderer in the Garden of Eden. Adam and Eve get to walk with God in a substantial and physical way. The disciples walk with Jesus in much the same way as the walks taken in Eden, minus Samaria (since skipping Samaria may have been something the disciples would have loved).

One day Adam and Eve are off by themselves rather than walking with God when they run into an unsavory character in the form of the serpent. Evidently unaware of stranger danger they engage in a conversation. I should clarify, Eve engages in a conversation. Before we turn this into an attack on Eve we should be careful to remember that Adam seems to be standing by like a lump. Nice work, Adam.

By the end of the conversation Eve takes the fruit that has been forbidden and she sees that it looks good. This really shouldn't come as a surprise as all of the fruit of the Garden would have looked good. What may be more important to grasp is that we always hope that the wrong choice will force us away, or seem unappealing, but that isn't often the case. Clearly if the fruit was all moldy, misshapen, worm infested, and rotting then no one would have eaten from that tree. Yet this was a "good" Garden, so all of it was created with beauty.

Just because something looks enticing doesn't mean it is right for you.

There are plenty of things in this world that are beautiful, but they aren't a part of the dreams and call on our life from God, and that means that they don't fit in our creative journey. Adam and Eve had this wide open creative space with wonderful and amazing things to do and participate in with God. Eve takes a bite and ventures off from God's desires, then she hands the fruit to a lump—I mean Adam—and he jumps in of his own accord.

By the end of the story Adam faces God, with a limited amount of beings in all of creation, and does his best to blame the serpent, Eve and God! If Adam hasn't lived up to his call and creative potential it is obviously the fault of everyone else. Unfortunately, the judgment doesn't go his way despite his rousing "blame everyone else" defense. Adam and Eve are cast out of the

Garden, and God for the first time shows mercy on sinners, thus beginning the restoration of all of creation, that once more all may be called "good."

The often misconstrued "Old Testament God of Wrath" has, from the first transgression, displayed patience, mercy, and spirit of reconciliation so that humanity may also be restored as "good" creation.

God will *fill* us up, not *use* us up

When our calling falls apart we accuse God of trying to destroy us. It happened in the Garden of Eden and it happens now. We often fall for the lie that our Creator designed us for the singular purpose of using us up until we're empty and dry. But in believing this we willfully choose to ignore the way that God prefers to be revealed in our lives. When Jesus is at Jacob's Well he refers to himself as having living water that we may no longer thirst, and when God speaks to Moses it is in a bush that isn't consumed by the fiery presence of God. That tends to catch your attention.

However, we forget about such imagery, and begin to forget about the revelation of God. See, the presence of God is a fire in the bush. Moses is drawn in, though, because the bush *is not consumed*, and the bush isn't consumed because God is self-sufficient and doesn't need to burn us up as fuel to exist. Moses is being shown that his life will have the fire of God present, and that as long as he is in that fire of God, he isn't going to be destroyed.

The bush is engulfed in flame, but the flame does not need the bush to exist. The bush is not significant except that it showcases the wonder of the flame. Period. This is why we cannot be burnt out and fully filled with the Spirit at the same time. Allowing the Spirit of God to reign in our lives means that we sing praises while we're shackled, we pray for bold perseverance when we're told that doing so will lead to death, and we are thrilled to be a prisoner in Rome because God promised we would one day be in Rome.

This is also what it means when we are told that we are a light. We are not the flame of the light, for that is the radiance of God at work in us. When we live in the creative freedom and blessing of being called and walking with our Caller we participate as a bush, engulfed in flame yet not consumed. Sure, we could seek some other source of beauty, some other source of light. But those flames would destroy us like the forbidden fruit in the Garden.

Not only does the flame of false light lead to our

destruction, but it is incredibly ineffective, as the world is used to burn-out. We see it all the time, and it isn't attractive or even interesting. Most of us are fading quickly under the flames, and we don't seem to notice what it means for us, or even that everyone else is doing the same thing. One thing is for sure, though. When the destructive flames we choose instead of God are revealed for what they are, not one of us would be interested in having them in our own lives.

Seeking to live a life apart from the Caller burns us up and we really are destroyed, but that isn't the will of God. Apart from a wandering, listening relationship with the Caller, the call atrophies and dies. To hear is to obey; to stay in the midst of the calling of God is to *keep* walking in obedience. But we do not walk alone. As the old chorus says, "He walks with me and He talks with me."

Not only that, but God even dances.

Chapter Three
When a Dance Partner Falls

Your life as a created being living with a call from God is a significant thing, and the ramifications of such a relationship are critical. An important thing to remember, though, is that the calling is a *relationship*. As I've mentioned before, when we come to a place of recognizing or realizing a call it is at a time of openness to the will of God. By some manner we can sense God at work in our lives. This means that we have been in a space most accommodating for growth.

Imagine, if you will, that you are a plant. The plant is set soundly in soil, directly in the light of the sun, and bountifully blessed with rain. That was what your life looked like when you were willing to say "yes." Now imagine if that plant decided to pull itself up from the soil, and crawl away to a dark shady place that receives no rainfall. How do you think that would work out? Not so well, right? That's because the plant has abandoned everything it needs to survive.

When our answer starts to become "no," then we are like that foolish plant. Our "no" to God's call is a failed transplanting and our refusal is typically *rooted* in what proves to be a lie about what is best thing for our life. Typically we spend a lot of time sore spiritually from trying to shield ourselves from the will of God when we perceive it to be painful. What we find in reality is that our roots are exposed and we are no more than tumbleweed, ready to be tossed about by the wind. The book of James warns us about this sort of doubt.

Now think of the sunlight as your fellowship with the Body of Christ, the rain as your time in the Word, and the soil as your continual life of prayer, because all three items work together. Sun, water, and soil combine to provide the fullest nourishment, the greatest security, and the most solid hope for life. Remove one and the other two become less effective; remove two and the remaining one becomes a mockery, so that long before you remove them all the chance for survival becomes a false hope.

What does this have to do with your calling, though? Like I said at the beginning, calling is a relationship. One of the biggest mistakes that a person can make is to accept a call from God and then rush off without God to make the calling happen. (You could probably substitute "biggest" in that previous sentence with "most common," too.)

I can't tell you how many colleagues I saw at the college level come in with a knowledge of a calling from God, then fall into a "life as usual" lifestyle where God ranged from afterthought to inconvenience, and then (sometimes) graduated with degrees in a field they no longer believed in or to which they no longer felt connected. The entire process became a mockery to the calling that had led them to that path because they thought *calling* was an event and not a relationship. So they attended the event, they accepted the invitation and they rushed off in search of a destination, when instead they had actually been welcomed to a journey with God.

Creation is commission

Throughout Genesis chapter one there is this cyclical occurrence that displays one of the first things we must acknowledge about God: God speaks a reality into existence—thereby creating it—and in doing so finds this work to be "good" and meeting His approval. All that God creates is "good" and nothing holds this "goodness" apart from the creative work of God.

Creativity requires obedience because our participation in creativity is to bring forth the reality that God seeks to speak through us.

The word "good" used there in the original Hebrew is a very rich word meaning that what was created is complete for the purpose it was designed to perform. Then God creates humankind in the image of God and also calls us, man and woman, "good." Wow, that's really loaded. Especially when we understand that we are created in the very image and likeness of God.

Sometimes it's hard for me when I have to address verses that tell me to be a blessing to God. I feel very small and unworthy in those moments and the task feels very big and overwhelming. Since God is so great and awe inspiring and I am not, I can become consumed with that rather than the fact that God takes great joy in getting to be my loving Father.

I went home recently and hanging next to my dad's chest of drawers was a poster with a sticker on it and some crudely handwritten message. I don't even recall how old I was when I created that marvel of mixed media, but based on the handwriting alone I can tell I was young. The poster hanging there is no coincidence, either, because we didn't even live where my parents live now when I made that piece of "art." When I see that piece now it strikes me as this goofy thing, and I wonder, "What was I thinking?" Yet, for dad it still means something. It was a gift, it was from his son, and it was pleasing to him. The gift was intended to bring him joy and in that regard the gift was "good."

Right after God created humankind He spoke to them and told them to increase, to be fruitful, to fill the land. Essentially they were being told to go off and have offspring. To make children, but these children would be disciples of the Lord. The incredible commission and call that they had was that just, as they knew the Lord and were called to obey the Lord as this new young humanity, they would then raise their offspring to do so as well.

What ended up happening was that in just a few generations the offspring no longer worshiped God — to such a degree that Noah and his family were the only ones to survive. God had been giving these general callings, though, from the beginning of time. These general, "this is the creative living that all humanity should do," type callings. One of the terrible things that can happen in the Church is that we adopt the creative-less concept that, in everyday life, our general callings look like everyone acting in exactly the same way and doing exactly the same things. That's just not the case. God is our shepherd so that we don't have to look like sheep following sheep. We're called to more!

Creativity in obedience to God is a matter of multiplying. Multiplying doesn't simply happen by persuading people into becoming homogenous converts. Rather multiplying happens by walking with people, by living life with them, being creative and doing so in a sense of community—not only in front of and open to others, but also *with* others.

Creative obedience will benefit more than just you.

The disciples that Jesus poured life and Spirit into left the upper room with different styles of worship because worship is life, and each one of them had a different life to live in obedience to God—though they all had the same focus of worship. Today we spend a lot of time trying to create different versions of God we want to worship while also trying to insist that people worship in a way that *we* find most pleasing.

Typically when we are called we try to form God's call in our life to fit our desires. One of the biggest parts of obedient creativity is allowing God to realign our dreams. Having dreams realigned may mean that we have to step out from the shadow of the *status quo* and trying to live out worship in the same way everyone else does. To follow the shepherd may mean we have a different trot and path then some of the sheep we want to emulate. Are we willing to obey when our path isn't the one we first envisioned?

Chapter Four:
Realigning the Dream

The story of Joseph is one of the most intriguing stories I can see in Scripture when speaking of creativity. Joseph had a few of the most significant traits required to have a creative life in obedience to God.

1) Joseph was incredibly aware of God's presence in everyday occurrences, such as dreams and opportunities.

2) Joseph was always willing to allow God to guide him into making a situation better.

3) Joseph didn't stop believing when things became difficult, frustrating, or inexplicably failed.

If you really look at Joseph's life there are elements there that will continue to change the course of attentive lives throughout history. He wasn't presumptive upon God to do things the way he expected them to turn out. Joseph's story began with him sharing two distinctly clear dreams, or so it seems. At the time his brothers were first upset because it seemed he thought they would bow to him. By the time he shares the second dream everyone—including his dad—got upset. The dreams that Joseph received, and openly shared, actually seem pretty cut and dried. Here is the problem with assumption and dreams.

Joseph was a descendant of Abraham, who God promised would be the father of a great, innumerable, nation. This was a promise understood to be passed down the bloodline. Isaac was promised much the same, with even more emphasis on the land in which his family was settling, and this continued to his sons, Jacob and Esau (we shouldn't forget that Esau's people also became a nation). Jacob's name was even changed by God to Israel, the name by which the nation would be known. Here's where our hindsight (being so seemingly clear) can cause us to miss something of significance: Joseph could have easily come to the conclusion that, as the heir to these familial promises, God was about to put him in charge of his family and the surrounding lands and peoples.

When you stop and think about that, you can see how the dream could get really dangerous very quickly. Suddenly those corrupt dreams of power might spring up—a ruling authority in an unstable land. The next thing you'd know, he's making an ill-advised move like a young Hitler, standing in a beer hall and proclaiming he is taking over the country. As it turns out, Hitler had over-estimated the level of disarray in Germany as the Germans not only *didn't* put him in charge, but also arrested him for his public idiocy. In his case it was a bad dream off to an embarrassing start (the finish wasn't any better).

Joseph, fortunately, didn't try to circumvent God's work in his life, but waited for the dreams God set before him to come to fruition, even if it wasn't what he expected.

We do our best for God

Have you ever noticed that everywhere Joseph went he ended up in charge? Not just over a few things, but literally in a position where the only person with more authority than Joseph wasn't actually *in charge* of more than Joseph. I've always found this pretty amazing. When Joseph was in Potiphar's house, he was in charge of everything happening in the house. Potiphar might have been the ultimate authority, but the truth is Potiphar tended to other things and let Joseph control his house so that he didn't have to be burdened by such matters.

When Joseph was in the jail he had more power than anyone else other than the jailer, whose authority was only positional in nature. Joseph was the one who made things work. Once more this repeated under Pharaoh as the most important work in all of Egypt was under Joseph's direction and all of the resources of Egypt moved under Joseph's command.

Now, have you ever thought about why? I truly believe it was because Joseph was a dreamer. Joseph didn't have the tendency to walk into a situation, shrug, and dismissively say, "Well, this works." No! Joseph looked at the things he did in the world as an opportunity to be pleasing to God, and that meant that just doing things well left room for doing things *better!*

Creativity in worship means that there is an ongoing thirst for righteousness. We don't want to simply do well for God, we long to give our best!

An aspect of going from well enough to better, and even better, and even better than that is insisting on realigning our dreams. A dream that becomes reality is no longer a dream. This is cause for great celebration, and at the end of this book we will talk at length about celebrating, but it isn't a cause for stagnation. Reaching one dream shouldn't create a spirit of apathy, but rather the pursuance of other dreams. Finishing one thing can be a great catalyst to finishing others.

Rolling through dreams
Sometimes I make to do lists. I was insane with

them when I was in school. It probably would have benefitted me to have more of the lists pertain to school, but there were many times that I would sit in a classroom and instead of doodling, I would begin to jot down a to do list.

With that sort of time on my hands those lists could get pretty elaborate. On top of that I had the bad tendency to date them so that each list was specific to that day. Later I would typically look at the list and feel completely overwhelmed. The perfectionism that caused me to write such an elaborate list was now the emergency brake I was slamming in my head by saying that I simply couldn't do everything to the level I desired.

Some days the list would be tossed on my desk in my room as a result. Other days it would be trashed, just to save time in cleaning the desk later. Yet many days I would pick one thing and absolutely *nail* it so that, with a big smile, I would take my pen and mark straight through the whole item. The result of that was scouring the list for another task. Check. Then another. Check. Soon I had knocked off multiple items and done them to a point where I was well pleased. Doing one thing beyond "well enough" to a place of "even better" was a catalyst for much more success throughout the day.

Allowing our dreams to continue to change can be a huge blessing. Yet there were some dreams that changed in ways that I hadn't desired or anticipated. Joseph would have experienced this in knowing that he would never be the great leader of his family's homeland. While that clearly remained a big part of his heart—because he asked that his remains be returned home some day—he had a dream he was actively living out, and it was also appropriate for him to grieve the loss of part of his dream so that he could accept the fullness of God's dream for his life. There was still great blessing, and he had saved the lives of all of his family, even if he didn't get to return home.

Grieving the dream
The summer before my junior year of high school I was at a church teen camp. Those days were exciting days in my life. I had been working diligently to raise my cumulative GPA at school and I was looking at getting a solid scholarship to a state school where I had every intention of studying writing and illustration. Between what I wanted to do graphically and my desire to tell stories I had hope that I could make a successful career in writing.

Everything was going great until Thursday night of that week. The speaker wasn't particularly great. In fact, I found myself largely distracted throughout the message. I grew frustrated and began a monologue in my head about how it was so clear that he was trying to manipulate us rather than letting God speak. I was growing more and more frustrated and cynical when I realized that I wasn't involved in a monologue at all. Rather, I was participating in a dialogue with God.

"Well I could do a better job than this guy. He's just trying to get everyone to react emotionally. He's barely even talking about God at this point."

"I agree. You could do better. In fact, with me, I think you could do great."

"Uh, what? Lord? What are you saying."

"I'm saying I'm calling you to youth ministry."

"But, Lord, I have a plan. I'm going to be a writer and illustrator. I'm going to go to a school I can easily afford and I'm going to use those skills."

There was silence for a while and I grew incredibly uncomfortable.

"Are you going to obey me or not?"

A big part of realigning a dream may be found in that very question. I've been asked that question too many times by God in my life. Still, I know what the answer needs to be. I knew the right answer then, as well.

"Yes, Lord, I'll obey you."

The next thing I knew I was at the altar. I was excited because I knew that I was doing what God desired of me and I had been promised that there was greatness in obeying, even if I didn't know what that would mean. However, I was very disappointed in that time, and throughout the following weeks, realizing that because I was going to be a youth pastor I would never get to be a writer.

Except, as I'm sure you've noticed, I have written this book you are reading. The problem with my dream was that it was all about me. The writing and illustrating I wanted to do were centered on making *my* name great and seeking attention for myself. God had promised me that there would be greatness if I obeyed, but what I couldn't grasp in that moment of adolescent arrogance was that God was beginning a work in my heart where the desire would be for *God's* name to be known and exalted as great. My job would simply be to let others know the good news of God at work rather than taking the credit.

I have yet to fully grasp all that I was being taught in those moments. My dream of writing went on a backburner for years. However, while pursuing my education to be a youth minister, I ended up in an English class where my professor insisted that I also make a point to further pursue my writing. God was already bringing about a restoration of writing in my life. What I assumed would have to be discarded completely actually needed to go through fire so that it could be refined and used for God's glory.

What I have learned is the importance of two things in our lives: the sacred nature of dreams, and that if something is meant to be sacred then it ultimately must be in God's hands. When God makes something sacred it is purified. We are baptized by the Spirit and fire. Fire was a refining and purifying tool in the Bible. When you read about fire it is typically destroying that which is unnecessary so that which is valuable remains.

I didn't realize at the time that I wasn't in a relational position with the Caller to be a writer. God wasn't closing the door on writing, but was telling me that it wasn't the right time.

God gives divine purpose to our dreams so we must trust in divine timing, too.

A dream can mean a lot. If we let the dream mean too much we can let it overtake us and our pursuit of the dream will become the means by which we are destroyed. When we are willing to allow God to refine and purify our dreams they may look drastically different when God is done with them, but they will be far more glorious for the work of the Kingdom. We must remember that the glory brought about by our dreams will only have a lasting value if it brings glory to God above and beyond us.

This is a different book
In the beginning I spoke about quitting a job so I could pursue writing. At that time there was a book I knew I was supposed to write. This isn't that book. That book is gone. I made my choices to disobey and I can't be certain that I will ever get to write that book now. There have been times, even recently, where I have picked up my notes for that book and read through them, or have looked at the few parts that I had begun to draft. But I no longer have any connection to that book. I don't doubt that God can restore that work, but I leave that in the Lord's hands. I'm thrilled that he restored the dream of writing.

As I just previously mentioned, writing has actually been a long term dream. The reason was so that I could do a comic strip, write children's books, create graphic novels, or whatever I felt would pour out. God had placed a certain level of skill, and a distinct passion, in my life for such things.

When I learned about my call to youth ministry I was so certain that writing had to be abandoned completely. Sometimes we have those thoughts. We throw the baby out with the bath water, as the old saying goes. In this instance the baby is our dream. I'm sure the bathwater is also something really deep, but for me it had to be my understanding of God. Thinking that God didn't want to use all of me—my passions, gifts, and life—was a grave error in my understanding.

God is not a wasteful Creator. You are designed with purpose. There is not one part of you that God can't restore and repurpose for the work of the Kingdom of Heaven.

The sign of Jonah

There came a point in Jesus' life and ministry where he had been providing many miraculous signs and wonders, yet the Pharisees came and demanded a sign that he was the messiah.

Christ, instead, offers them only the "sign of Jonah." Some argue that what Christ is saying there is that, like Jonah was in the belly of the big fish for three days, Christ will be in the "belly of the earth" for three days before returning. It's a weak argument, though. What I *do* believe Christ is speaking about is the nature of Jonah's heart in response to the signs of God during Jonah's ministry. That discontented nature was also present in the generation of that day—and, I fear, in today's generation—as well.

Jonah's ministry revolved around obedience to God, and the real struggle Jonah had was a matter of pride. Pride determined that Jonah had a better notion of what his ministry should look like than God did.

Never confuse pride in yourself as anything other than fear acting out.

When Jonah does finally obey God and go to Nineveh he pronounces that God will act against the sinful people of Nineveh. When God acts it is a **SIGN**! Jonah desires for God to act—he probably even hopes that these people will receive worse than Sodom and Gomorrah for the atrocious acts they have committed. Jonah isn't just demanding a sign in his heart; he is demanding a specific sign.

And God does *not* deliver!

This is grace. For us to realign the dream we must also accept God's grace.

The Pharisees and others gathered who demand a sign from Christ have the same mindset. They want what they think is best for their lives. The signs they seek are political power, nationalistic pride and the outright embarrassment of those with dominion over them as they are shamed, defeated and driven out of their land. The Messiah was supposed to bring about the restoration of their nation, and they want it at all costs against all opposition.

Christ refuses. He comes to offer grace. He comes to be a blessing to Israel and to anyone else, even the Roman Empire. He brings hope to *all* people, not just the people of his birth and heritage. They want God to act, they want a sign, and this will happen, but not to the desire of their hearts. The sign they receive will be one that leaves them angry, because they aren't looking for God's grace to be at work in their life. They are certain they have a better plan.

If there is only one thing you take away from this book make it this: Nothing will destroy the glorious freedom of creative reverence and obedience more thoroughly than demanding a lesser sign than the one God wants to offer.

God's grace is sufficient! Our humbled hearts must be willing to accept the sign we receive over the sign we desire.

Even recently, God has stressed this to me and shown me the error of my ways and desires. I can't adequately express the heartache and tears poured out over the revelation that I was willfully defying God because I desired lesser signs and refused to rejoice when God acted benevolently for others as well as on my behalf.

Chapter Five:
Repentance and the Life After

One thing I have run into so many times I can't even begin to count is the story of regret that comes with someone telling me about the true call God placed in their life and how they eventually turned from it, leaving it unfulfilled. Whether it was the first song an artist asked for that wasn't submitted before the deadline, the article that was never written when the query for publication was accepted, or the idea that could have turned things around for the business that ended up going under—in all of these stories, there is one thing that remains similar: there was a distinct urge to do something that wasn't done, and the end result is a continued remorse.

In the last chapter, we spoke about grieving a dream so that it could be realigned. The final stage of grief is acceptance, and accepting that a dream will not turn out how we anticipated is a necessary matter—as is accepting when we are responsible for that happening.

The mere acceptance of responsibility alone is a tragic thing, though. Ending at that point leaves an open door to beat yourself down over your past shortcomings for the rest of your life. Each time you are faced with the joyous opportunity to step into a dream the reminder will come that you have previously destroyed your dreams to the point where you believe that all dreams you have will be squandered. This will balloon into something intended to steal, kill and destroy both you and your dreams as the enemies of the Kingdom of God will work diligently to persuade you — through lies — that you are unfit to do Kingdom work.

The sin of omission
Over the course of the numerous discussions I've had with well-intentioned Christians, it has become evident that many are frustrated with the status of their life in the midst of the calling God has given. Time and time again I hear about how, at one point in time, there was a decision to be made where the individual knew that to do something was God's will, but they chose another path.

Such an action is a sin of omission, for we have failed to obey. The confession of such sins doesn't seem to really cross the minds of many people today, though, as the Church has often been so focused on pointing out the many "do not's" of Christianity. When we cross the line of a "do not" sin and do it anyway there is a pain that reminds us we will need to be healed. The same is true for the pain of *not* doing those things we *should* do. We need to be healed and restored in Christ in order to have the strength for obedience when we are again called upon by God.

Repentance is a significant occurrence in the process of creative obedience. Repentance is where the individual participates in God's desired restoration of all of creation. When we repent, we participate in an event that is intended to be a continual transformation from here forward.

Addiction to disobedience
As a minister, one of the most ironically intriguing conundrums I run into when working with individuals is a combination of two opposing thoughts: all are willing to admit they have probably sinned (it's pretty much a cultural given at this point, so why fight it?), yet most deny that they are doing anything wrong. If you fail to see how that works, I understand your struggle because it always leaves me baffled.

Here's how the thought process of the "sin free sinner" typically works out in their minds. Sinning is doing something they don't want to do, or not doing something they want to do. Because of that they have sinned. So all they have to do is convince themselves that everything they do is something they *want* to do and they are no longer living any sort of wrongdoing, since our society has tried to ingrain that your personal choice is okay with few to no exceptions.

All of this wishful thinking—but ultimate abuse—of our lives is far more conveniently accomplished when God is entirely left out of the equation. However, the effect of this is that gifts that are designed to bring God glory cannot be fully realized and accomplished—whether they are used or abandoned—sinfully. Trying to use your gifts apart from God is like being blessed with a rocket, but not having any rocket fuel. As awesome as it looks, the end result is empty and futile.

Worse than having a flightless rocket is the callousness that leads to being content to see the rocket every day and not worry about the fact that it's being completely wasted. There is a real sickness in sin, and we as humans aren't so compartmentalized that what happens in our spiritual lives can go on without impacting our mental, emotional, physical, and relational lives. Instead, the spiritual battle of disobedience eventually becomes the psychological battle of disconnectedness. We start to "check out" of our own lives. Saying no to God hurts. To damage a relationship is painful. In self-defense we try to separate ourselves from that pain by ceasing to address the matter. Soon we have a decaying relationship with God on one side, and a prepared system of walls to keep from feeling that pain on the other side—all because we chose at some point to say no to God's will for our lives.

Even David ran from God

There are times where running from God doesn't look very much like running at all. While Jonah hopped on a boat and tried to sail out in the opposite direction of his intended destination, most of our running looks more like blatant obstinance. The writer of 2 Samuel begins the eleventh chapter with such an accusation against David. In fact, it's a pretty scathing commentary on the king, because when kings like David should have been out leading the army in battle, David sent others out to do that while he remained behind in the comforts of the palace and Jerusalem.

Unfortunately, that's only the beginning of David's poor choices. Soon he saw something he liked—one of the soldier's wives, Bathsheba—and decided to claim her as his own. That really escalated quickly. The story never seems to get better. Each new action of David's from that first point of inaction leads to results that are even more devastating than the previous ones. Lives are lost, hearts are broken, David hardens toward God and won't listen to anyone until the prophet Nathan effectively catches him through some misdirection so he can finally face the truth.

All too often we think that if we disobey God it is a little thing that will only hurt us, and we hope that grace will cover it over. Instead what tends to happen is we open our hearts to travel on a journey of continued disobedience leading to much destruction in our lives and the lives of others.

Running from God results in arriving where God would not want us. We can often see the creative calling as too great a challenge and want to hide, but it is a calling of love. Being called to where God would love for us to be is the *best place* in each season of our lives.

David probably felt like he was playing it smart. A king in battle could be put at great risk. He wasn't a young warrior anymore, so he was willing to let the young warriors do the dirty work for him. Yet what he did was displeasing and even as his army was victorious there were great losses beginning to accumulate in the wake of his disobedience.

Instead, what may have seemed like the best move based on worldly wisdom was absolutely the worst move for David. This is a major reason why the "to-do" list isn't something I can populate for you in this book. The formulas don't work, and even if I'd found an incredible path to success once, that wouldn't guarantee it would be my path to success the next time, much less mean that you would find any success that way.

What is clear is that David wasn't acting in step with God's design for his life. The criticism is sound from the one documenting the story because the way it plays out makes it clear that David had lost sight of *why* he was called to be king, which was that he had a heart after the heart of his God—the King Most High.

So strong, so wrong
When I was in college working toward the calling God had placed on my life, I entered into a deep depression because of a broken heart. Now I need to make this clear—depression is not sin, but it will only be compounded by disobedience to God. In the midst of my depression, and trying to self-medicate, I threw myself into a lot of things that, in and of themselves, weren't bad. I began to spend a lot of time with friends, grew very focused on athletics and fitness, was intently focused on my diet, enjoyed movies, and completely betrayed the Caller and my calling. Well, that last one would definitely be bad.

In that season of my life I had been hurt in a relationship. I had allowed that relationship to become an idol. When it dissolved I didn't turn back to God, I turned to things that made me feel good. Still, I figured that I knew the right formula to good living, so I avoided drugs and illegal activities. Instead I became distinctly focused on some form of self-improvement. I began spending hours playing soccer, working out, and playing basketball each day. My entire diet catered to my athletic pursuits. I also became more culturally well-rounded by watching many critically acclaimed movies with some friends. I was determined to be a better man.

At first it all felt safe, it made sense to the world and it looked good on me. People had noticed by the time I only had 6% body fat. I was trim and athletic. Clearly this would make me happier. I looked good in the mirror and I was excelling at the sports I chose to participate in by having more endurance than almost anyone I faced. While it was all recreational, it soothed my competitive nature.

The big problem was that my life was empty and I was trying to fill it with things that, if they had to be my purpose, begin to feel meaningless very quickly. While I was winning a lot at what I did, I stopped caring entirely. None of it was a good enough reason to get up in the morning. I had stopped talking to God and learning about him, including skipping most of my classes that semester. By the end I only managed to pass one. I was walking away from the Caller, seeking comfort, and hoping that finding something that "worked" could replace living in right relationship.

Like David I was doing all of the wrong things. While he was supposed to be king and I was supposed to be at the university I was attending, neither of us were doing those things the right way. We'd chosen a different path right in the middle of the journey. Having departed from the God who is faithful to complete the good works started in us we had opened ourselves up to great danger.

Repentance can't be about trying to find a formula that works. We are too susceptible to picking the wrong things, too prone to fall for temptation, and too proud (and simultaneously foolish) to reach the greater "good" to which we were called by God. Even trying to become legalistic about things is a pitfall because God holds us to a standard of relational justice, not legalism.

Relational justice means that God judges us by our heart toward him, not the means by which we follow a list of rules. Now, to be fair, if we blatantly ignore what God says is best for us then there is clearly rule-breaking. Beyond that, though, is the greater issue of being disobedient and in poor relationship with God. We lose sight of our covenant of love with God where our repentance says, "Because I love you, I will live for you." When we lose sight of this covenant love, we also lose sight of who we are, because we can't know *who* we are unless we remember *Whose* we are.

Chapter Six:
Humility Trumps Self Esteem

David seemed to run into pride issues as the king of Israel. Pride is a common issue. Our calling becomes about us and we begin to make it our identity, rather than letting the Lord form our identity and, likewise, shape our calling continually. There have been times when I have believed that a calling was synonymous with me. In those moments my calling was no longer God's, it was mine—and all about me.

I *am* important. I know from Scripture this is true. However, my importance is directly linked to two things if we are to take Christ's affirmation of the two-part "greatest commandment" seriously—that God is the sole focus of love from *all* of me, and that the love built up within me in return is the same amount of love by which I love my neighbor.

God, having filled us with the understanding of how we are loved and cherished, helps us to humbly love our neighbor. What is clear is that knowing we are important to God is not a pride issue—rather it will help us love others. But when we begin to think we are important *apart* from God, our pride will lead us to acts that are truly dangerous.

Perhaps no one knew this better than Nehemiah. Maybe one of my favorite lines in all of Scripture is a response Nehemiah has to a dangerous situation. At first it reads full of pride, except that Nehemiah's understanding of *who* he was found its value in knowing to *Whom* he belonged.

Let me explain. Nehemiah was a captive in Babylon during the time of exile. He was King Artaxerxes' cupbearer. Now, while he did work for the king, this wasn't quite as lofty a position as we may think. Nehemiah was still a slave in captivity — a man heartbroken because he wasn't in the hurting land he still understood as home — to do the bidding of the king who reigned over his people against their will.

Not only that, but the position meant that Nehemiah was basically the food and drink crash test dummy. The cupbearer had to partake of whatever the king desired during his meals *before* the king would have any. Nehemiah ate first, but it wasn't lofty, it was so the king could keep an eye on him and make sure he wasn't poisoned. Ah, the prestige!

Nehemiah knew he was a slave to the king. Nehemiah knew that his position could lead to his death if someone wanted to poison the king, but he also knew that fleeing from his position would be considered the act of a traitor and he would be hunted down and killed. When you really look at it what you see is that the potential for death surrounds Nehemiah daily. Stay or leave, he could die soon, and he remained and was faithful to the king.

Then Nehemiah got bad news. Jerusalem, the capital of his homeland, was without walls and wide open to roving bandits on a nightly basis. The people were terrified, taken advantage of, and distraught. When Nehemiah heard this he was visibly shaken and heartbroken. Suffice it to say the king found very little comfort in seeing his cupbearer looking out of sorts. Eventually Nehemiah was forced to admit his heartache because Artaxerxes started to get that ill feeling in the pit of his stomach that if Nehemiah looked like such a mess he may be next. Nehemiah admitted that his heart was broken because Jerusalem needed a wall Artaxerxes had pity and sent him—the cupbearer—to lead the wall building efforts.

Nehemiah took the task seriously, knowing that it was clearly God who had opened such doors. Cities defeated by Babylon were not allowed to have walls because being able to remain fortified might have led the people of the city to do something foolish, like believe they could revolt against their captors. So "wall builder" wasn't exactly at the top of anyone's résumé. Nehemiah—the cupbearer—was as qualified as anyone else for the task based on experience. He was most qualified, though, because God had called him. Nehemiah understood the successful completion of the calling to be his service to the God Most High. Again, Nehemiah understood that *who* he is rests upon knowing *Whose* he is, and while Artaxerxes held him as a captive slave, it was the Lord who held Nehemiah's heart.

Any time we accept our calling it seems that there are naysayers looking to come along and destroy the work. Nehemiah had a few and they were the worst of the worst. Not only did they want Nehemiah to fail, they wanted him dead! A few plans had already died when they hatched a beauty of one. They tried to get Nehemiah to move from his post by making him believe that if he stayed where he was he would die and that safety would be found by running into the Temple. Of course they planned to ambush him in the Temple, but it did make the most sense to leave that part out of the message they sent to Nehemiah.

Nehemiah's response was incredible: "Should a guy like me *run away*?" Their whole plan was turned upside down because Nehemiah's humble understanding of who he was kept him at his post. If running from Artaxerxes would lead to death, then it was better to take his chances as the cupbearer. Now Nehemiah saw the Lord, who was even more powerful than Artaxerxes, as the one he served, and he would not leave his post and face the wrath of God. He would remain faithful to his Caller and his calling.

When we are appointed by God we don't need to shy away from the fact that it is *God* who sees us as significant. We should honor that tenaciously! Nehemiah was even less interested in leaving this post than he would have been to leave his work in Babylon. To him, abandonment was *always* death. When he spoke of himself in this way, it was not a self-appointed arrogance, but rather a humble servant mentality. God had appointed him to a task and a "man such as" Nehemiah is a man who has value in his active obedience. That sort of man, or woman, is the type of person who understands that the God who created him/her as "good" is also the God who speaks the truest "good" into his/her life!

We can lose sight of calling through pride and try to make what is good in it about us, but then it isn't the sort of "good" that is breathed from the Creator of the universe. We can also lose sight of calling through a misappropriation of humility, where we instead break down the "good" spoken into our lives by being self-deprecating rather than truly humble. There is no worship, no glorifying God, in doing such things. We can appropriately point the value of what we do back to God's provision, but to act as though we're unworthy of the task is to call God a liar, since it is God who speaks such worth into our lives.

So take a deep breath. Remember you are called, and that a called person doesn't run away, a called person doesn't flee (which, as with Nehemiah, is where death is waiting). Go to a mirror and look at yourself and remember that the Creator of the universe, who breathes life into your lungs, has appointed you to your calling—speaking that worth into your life—and that means that a man/woman such as you should NOT run away!

Stolen identities

There are plenty of people who are willing to rob us of the identity the Caller gives. Our identity is not synonymous with our calling. As I stated previously, we probably don't have one singular calling, because we are called into a truly nuanced relationship. Since our calling is to the relationship with God, our identity is found as participants within the whole Bride of Christ.

Nehemiah faced three such identity thieves: Sanballat, Tobiah, and Geshem. They weren't pleased because they believed they were going to miss out. Unfortunately, they were leading a large number of others in opposition to Nehemiah, since Nehemiah's success didn't guarantee their success. The world often responds this way to the creative calling. Even worse, the world can often be found within the communities of those who claim to believe in the Caller.

Sanballat, Tobiah, and Geshem began a smear campaign. Their desire was to slander Nehemiah so someone else would keep him from doing what he should do. They even tried to get Artaxerxes to turn his back on his promise to Nehemiah. It didn't stick. They got furious and plotted death against Nehemiah, which we just talked about earlier in this chapter. Nehemiah never flinched in the face of any of this because of his closeness to the Caller.

The enemy of our souls, and those of the world who are his children (see 1 John 3), try to steal our identities. We are labeled as losers, failures, too little, too much, and pretty much wrong in all ways. We're told that the calling is stupid, or that we'll never do it well enough. The world heaps pain on us as a reflection of the pain it wears for its disobedient refusal to participate in the work of creating the "good" to which the Caller beckons. While the world doesn't realize it, this is part of all of creation groaning for the restoration found in the returning Savior.

Unfortunately the world offers weak facsimiles of the true "good" in which it was originally created. Emphasis is distorted toward the creation rather than the Creator. If we're not careful, we can even become lost in believing in the beauty of what we create more than understanding it as an act of worship.

Nehemiah, though determined to build the wall, wasn't lost on that singular task. Not only was he undeterred from building the wall by those who slandered him, he was also open to the fact that various callings can pop up in life. As he worked, he made sure that those in need were treated well. And so he transitioned from cupbearer to wall-builder to governor of Jerusalem with a steadiness that could only be found in resting in God's strength above and beyond his own.

When we're called to the creative there is a fluidity that must happen. So our identity can't be captured in the *thing* we are doing, but in the Caller with whom we are *journeying*. While slander and other attacks can easily derail our work when our focus is on the task at hand, we do have the option to stand strong in the presence of the Caller.

I don't know what the Sanballats, Tobiahs, and Geshems are in your life, but I do know that whether they are internal (your own fears, insecurities, apprehensions, etc.) or external (those who cast doubts, seemingly insurmountable odds, general negativity, or outright attacks), journeying hand in hand with the Caller can save you from having your identity—and your callings—stolen from your grasp. When we hold our calling by holding onto the hand of the Caller, we have active faith and the strength to keep our identity. When we let go of the Caller's hand, all may be lost, including ourselves.

Mustard seed faith
Perhaps one of the most telling things in Jesus' speaking about the mustard seed of faith is his acknowledgement of the perversion of the present generation, how "twisted" they are in their faithlessness. He is tired of their perversion of the concept of faith. They have lost sight of that which is God's and that which is for humankind to hold. Yet I wonder if we are much better.

So often I have heard well-meaning ministers and Christians speak of *having* more faith with some sort of strange economic bent to the concept. As though there is a place where we can buy up stock in faith and accumulate it for a gentle retirement, or just a rainy day. Yet there is something far more disconcerting about this rainy day faith. See, along with its mighty accumulation, the hope is that it will entitle us to the good things we seek from God. Perhaps, even, we can then take our persuasive faith and our sincere righteousness to coerce God to bend to our will!

Of course I know that no one would want to say it *that* way. Yet you'll hear it said that if you believe with all of your heart God will give you those desires. Or that if you pray in *true* faith that you will receive! There seem to be some critical omissions in these teachings, some omissions that may keep them from being Gospel.

For one thing, our faith is not the bully stick we wield to beat the Almighty God into submission to our will and desires. We can't, despite our best intentions, ever *force* God to act. Of course I've tried, and maybe you have, too. Praying with so much "faith" that we're willing to bargain *anything* to get what we want!

Another issue, though, is that we can't have a quantifiable amount of faith. I know Jesus said we must have faith as a mustard seed. However, he did not say this as a possessive type of having. So often we lose sight of what it means to "have" something in God's presence.

God is the holder of all good things—faith, hope, love, kindness, goodness, faithfulness, etc. We are **not** the holders of these things. We don't have an entitlement to them. We don't have a receipt of purchase. We don't have a legal right that means that our possession of faith equals our acquisition of what we insist upon.

I was trying to think of how to adequately display the difference between having (possession) and having (potential access) yesterday morning while getting my kids into the school building during drop-off. My three year old son was having a hard time keeping the pace. I reached out my hand and he, trusting me to guide him where he should go, reached up to grasp my hand.

In that moment he did not suddenly own my hand. It was still of me. Faith is still of God. Rather, he had full access to my hand and the benefits thereof.

One thing about holding the hand of my three year old son is that I don't wish to do him any harm. This means that my grip tends to be somewhat relaxed so that if he needs to let go he can do so without my damaging his arm. Especially the young, tender joints at the elbow and shoulder which can easily be injured at that age by a solid tug from an adult.

As a father I don't want to hurt my son, yet if he applies just a little pressure I can hold his hand in such a way that he can increase his pace and keep up with me. So he squeezes his little fingers around the edge of my hand, from the crook of my thumb all the way to the first knuckle of my index finger, so I can keep him safe.

There have been times where he has lost his balance and chosen to let go. In those instances he has crashed to the ground of his own choosing and has come up with skinned knees, scraped hands, and plenty of tears. Yet there have been other times where his potential plummet was averted by gripping into my hand more firmly, and as he had access to my hand I tightened my grip and lifted him ever so gently, yet firmly, so that he remained unharmed from potentially crashing to the ground.

When we make faith a possession and entitlement we place it up against God and allow a few things to happen. First, we try to trap God with all potential guilt. If our faith doesn't heed the result we desire, God has failed us and is to be blamed. God must be a bad God. Second, we put a value on the strength of our faith. If our prayers aren't answered, we must not have possessed the level of a teeny tiny little mustard seed worth of faith. Failure to acquire what we desire can send us hurtling into a crisis point. Third, we are constantly trying to acquire something that is not quantifiable by our measure. We can't grasp levels of faith. This is why God holds out to us the necessary faith for a given situation that we can potentially access, if we're willing to wrap our little fingers around tightly! Finally, we think we can have, or not have, faith. We actually begin to believe that we could walk away from faith or not possess it at all. "Well, I just don't have faith anymore." This is just not the case. Faith in our lives is accessible because of the grace of God. We cannot escape the presence of faith that can form and change us anymore than we can escape the love of God that is furiously present with a deep pursuit of us, God's beloved. Faith is ever present even when we are defiant of that presence. It was never ours to own and it is never ours to disown. Faith is of God, and where God is faith will be ready for us.

Faith is a matter of holding on, from the giving of a promise to the completion of that work. Faith is a journey in which we must hold tightly. Yet, with little fingers and tiny hands, it is critical to understand that it is God who carries the brunt of the burden of faith.

The burden of faith that we carry in comparison is that of a mustard seed—while God moves trees and mountains to bring Divine promises to fruition! God is reaching out the hand of faith that we might take hold—not to own, but to cling. This is promised, and God brings promises to reality.

Chapter Seven:
Speaking in Faith

Before he was King David—abstaining from doing what he should be doing during the time when kings went out to war—he was David the shepherd boy, sent solely to bring food to his brothers in Israel's army. While I won't spell out the entire story (you can find it in 1 Samuel 17), there are some interesting things I want to touch on that tie us back to the Genesis 1 creation.

In the beginning we find a God who just speaks and creation forms in such a way that it is deemed, by God, as "good." If we are open to such speech, we can see that God is speaking continually into our lives to form that which is "good." David arrives at the army encampment already open to such speech. So he speaks up for himself among the men of the army, which leads to him standing before King Saul, again speaking of his potential as a warrior, and finally he arrives on the battlefield—dressed as a shepherd—to face Goliath, where he once more speaks.

I truly love this passage of the Bible—it's one of a few instances of "holy trash talk," and David doesn't hold back. Goliath yells at him and mocks him. Up to this point, Goliath's mockery has led to some pretty solid results. Day after day, he has been walking out to this spot and bellowing insults to the entire army of Israel, that one soldier would come out and face him. Day after day, the army of Israel—from the weakest man all the way to King Saul—has cowered away from this monster of a man and his bold threats against them and their God.

Yet out steps young David, and as Goliath bellows out his mockery, David becomes a mouthpiece for God. David gets very specific in his response, in fact. Here are the key points:

1) You have spoken against God—I come in God's name.

2) Today you will be given to me by God.

3) I will strike you down and cut off your head.

4) The dead bodies of your army will be food for the birds and beasts.

5) *Everyone* will know that God is alive and well in Israel.

6) The LORD doesn't need swords or shields, and the battle *is* the LORD's.

David isn't shooting from the hip when he lobs

his reply to Goliath. He is echoing the Caller, who is giving final warning to a giant who is—next to the Caller—quite small. What Goliath misses is that David's threats are all offered with the *creative power* of the Caller. This is where Goliath—like the army of Israel so many times before—should refuse to engage the battle. Instead, he begins lumbering toward David.

Following the shepherd
For humankind, our creative nature is the echo of the Creator's call. Perhaps David had a better grasp of this than most because he was a shepherd in Israel. While most sheep herding techniques these days include driving the sheep like cattle, the shepherds of Israel would call to the sheep to guide them.

Such calling is the very thing Jesus is speaking of in John 10. The difference between the deceptive thief who comes to steal, kill and *destroy*, and the Shepherd—whose voice is recognized by the sheep—is that same polar difference between destruction and creation. While David's words are brutal and terrifying, he is echoing the Caller. Just as sheep would bleat and follow behind the call of their shepherd, now David is falling in step with the Caller that he may gain that which is most important.

David's approach to this battle is different and

creative. However, it's not *entirely* new, because above all else his approach to fighting Goliath is being *faithful* to the Caller. David's threats are truly the Caller's response. Every day the Caller was mocked by the giant, and on this day the Caller responds. What David is doing is participating in worship. David praises his Caller throughout his threat, for it is only by the mighty power of the one who calls David that he will succeed. David isn't making claims of his own. Rather he's pronouncing the creative vision of his Shepherd.

Our greatest victories are not our victories to claim. It is God who will give those giants we face over into our hands. For those who create, this is a mirroring of David – we approach the battle with a most unique set of weapons and a distinct message to bring.

Where walls crumble

The story of the battle of Jericho is so unique, so amazing, that we can easily miss that it is actually the first battle of a series of battles for the people entering the land promised to them. Like David would do generations later, Joshua steps into battle in a most unique manner. Joshua's words are the Caller's words, and the actions of the army of the children of Israel are the ascribed actions of the Caller.

As creative people, we can easily fall in love

with the story of David, or the story of Jericho, because we've experienced one great moment of creative brilliance that has forever changed our lives. Yet we can just as easily betray our calling Shepherd and try to wander off doing the same thing we'd done before rather than acknowledging that it is now time to do a new thing.

What's the problem with being formulaic? To be blunt, it'll get you slaughtered. For the children of Israel there could only be one battle of Jericho. Why? Because a victory like that means that word will spread. There won't be another city you can walk around for seven days without making any sort of military move. The next city will have already heard about what you did and they will attack you early on to avoid the same fate.

David had many military victories in his life. There's no record of him making the same sort of speech to a giant ever again. Part of speaking in faith is that we may be led to say different things at different times. God will lead us to different situations. Just like realigning the dream to the will of the Caller, we also need continual alignments to make sure that each new day is still in step with the Caller.

There is a balance to be struck. The words David

speaks as he echoes the Caller are words he knows he'll need to act out. Likewise, he will not speak those same words every time he goes to battle. Part of the beauty of the creative soul is that it is constantly seeking more creation. We don't simply make one thing "good," we face many situations that can go from "good enough" to the sort of "better" that is the true sense of "good" as designed by the Caller. We'll never make this sort of progress if we insist on approaching each new thing by our strength using an old stencil once offered to us by the Caller.

While that would be convenient, it would also deter us from the sort of worship-filled living that results in the Caller being the muse and the focus of our creative process. Instead, we would become self-absorbed and formulaic. Then praising the Caller would be abandoned for the purpose of seeking praise. Since it worked before we would want to rub that genie's bottle over and over again hoping for the same magical results.

Our faithfulness is not only a matter of running to complete the task set before us, but also understanding that the next journey we take may go in a different direction at an entirely different speed.

Chapter Eight:
Running in Faith

Returning to the story of David and Goliath, something incredible happens as the giant begins to lumber toward the shepherd boy. David's response is to *run* headlong into the battle. You can almost hear the audible groan of the army of Israel. The agreement to this battle was that the victorious warrior's army would enslave the opposing army. Watching the armorless and virtually unarmed David walk out to wage war against the massive and extremely armed Goliath had to cause a tremendous sinking feeling in the chests of many of Israel's bravest men.

Now, not only were they about to become slaves, but the foolish boy was running headlong to his defeat! They would surely become slaves—and *quickly*. Except David was taking the strides that he was called to take, living out the very message given to him by the Caller. David begins running and brings out a stone to place in his sling. On the sprint he launches this stone toward the giant. This would be a great time to admire the shot. However, that wasn't the end of what the Caller had commissioned David to do. So instead of stopping David's feet keep churning. As the stone sinks in and the giant falls to the earth, the shepherd boy continues to run on.

For the creatively inspired, becoming consumed with our first signs of victory may lead us to forget to keep running.

No bull, right relationship is key
One of my favorite things to do as a kid was ask my father to tell family stories at bedtime. He told stories of his childhood, which I enjoyed, but he also told many stories from our family that had been handed down to him. Learning about grandparents, great-grandparents and other distant relatives was incredible.

There are a few particular stories that have stuck with me that I find myself sharing from time to time. One is a story about my grandfather and his dad. Grandpa knew that when great-grandpa told him something, he was expected to hear and obey immediately. That was a hard and fast rule that wasn't meant to be tested.

One day when grandpa was a boy he was out playing in the field at the family farm. Great-grandpa came to the door and called him by name and instructed, "Come here!" Without hesitation, grandpa transitioned from hearing to obeying and left the field he was playing in, making his way through the fence, and on toward the house.

Just then the neighbor's bull, which had gotten into the field, came charging through in a rage where my grandpa had been playing only seconds before. Not only did grandpa's obedience lead him to a better place, it also saved him from great harm.

Throughout the Scripture we find a phrase that roughly insists, "If you have ears to hear then act and obey." To hear the Shepherd and echo is one thing, but we must also fall in step for the journey, and the greatest blessings come from holding to the Caller through the completion of the task.

Run on for others
In the previous chapter I listed a few things that David had yelled to Goliath. Had he only persisted until the stone took the giant to the ground and then stood there admiring his victory from afar he would have shortchanged the Caller. Not only that, but he would have also shortchanged himself. Oh, right, and then there's the fact that he would have shortchanged all of Israel and even the surrounding nations, who the Caller had promised through David would know of the might of God in Israel. It's far too easy for us to think quitting only hurts us, but this is far from the truth.

When I read the story, I can see the dust kicking up from David's sandals as he pursues the total victory. As I mentioned before, it's good to read the Bible with your imagination turned on. Seeing that dust in my mind, the eyes of both armies grow wide as the giant's eyes go lifeless, and for a second you can just feel the air leave the valley. No one on either side is breathing. The armor bearer for the giant is frozen in time as his master crashes to the ground with the tremendous thud of his weight and the extreme amount of armor and weaponry he could bear. And there is nothing more but silence, perhaps the light sound of the breeze kicking through, and one more thing—footsteps. Fast, intentional, and driving footsteps of a shepherd boy running headlong toward the fullness of victory for his task is not yet finished.

As he gets closer, David's eyes narrow with focus. The armor bearer hasn't even moved as the boy crashes by him with his hands extended toward the hilt of the giant's sword. Since even King Saul's sword had been too bulky and awkward for the boy, this sword can't even be explained as awkward in his hands. Yet he is fulfilling the creative mission of the Caller, and only David has been tied into this sort of creative vision until this moment. So everyone else stares on without breath, without motion, while the sword is hoisted over his head and the full weight of it relieves the giant's shoulders of their burden. As David lifts the massive head the air comes back, a giant inhale of something new, fresh, and inspired in the army of Israel. This is followed by the stark exhale of a victory cry as they began to move like a crashing wave across the valley to the utterly terrified Philistines.

What we can easily lose sight of as we run this race with endurance is that others will see us at work. The trials, the hardships, the crushing defeats, and the moments when faith feels impossible to muster (because we're trying to possess it on our own rather than clinging to the Caller who holds it all) are all instances where we are being led forward in our creative journey—and others *are watching*.

There is tremendous worship potential for the entire community when victories are reached. Doing something creatively at the behest of the Caller draws others into the desire for that same sort of relationship and response. When we remember that worship is about how we live our lives—not what we do for an hour on the weekend—then we can find that the experiential nature of it isn't so much a thing to shun, but rather like breathing.

While the onlookers hold their collective breath seeing the battle unfold, we must run on to the completion of the task in step with how the Caller desires and empowers, so that others may join in the victory!

Chapter Nine:
Worship is a Many Splendored Thing

An ongoing conversation I've had with my pastor is that if we are going to "pray always," as Paul encouraged the church in the first letter to the Thessalonians, then we need to pray *all ways*.

For me that sums up worship. Worship is life. Worship is living in and breathing God. In all the things we do, in all the ways we create, in every aspect of our being, there is space for worship when we make the adoration of God our primary purpose. Because of this, we must acknowledge that being created toward the end of worship opens up many means by which we'll meet that goal.

I'm afraid that there has been an abuse of the passage from First Corinthians (12:12-27) where Paul speaks of the Body of Christ, the Church, in a metaphorical sense. Somewhere along the line those of us who are a part of this Body began to believe we were only supposed to have one purpose. At church it often means people find one thing to do and they cling to it as though all of their Christian identity is stored in that one task. Or else they get so sick and tired of it they're not so sure the whole "faith" thing was really panning out.

I have always failed to see that as the main point, though. I doubt that Paul, the apostle-missionary that made it all the way to Rome spreading the good news of Christ, felt this way since he was a tentmaker during his journeys. This former Pharisee was both earning a wage as he traveled and yet also bringing a great message of hope. He knew he could contribute more than one thing to the world. We should know this, too.

In fact, Paul probably saw the Body of Christ as a collection of individuals who each contributed *multiple* things to the greater whole. I'd like to believe he thought of it more like this: perhaps God made us too great to be single-purpose cells. Perhaps we have more purpose than just one task. Perhaps—just maybe—being part of the Body points out that being called to be a thumb allows others to know they've done a good job, hails a ride when stuck on the side of the road, and partners with four other friends to help them get a grip.

One thing we're missing is that we live in a post-industrial revolution culture. So cities have become mega cities and conveniences are the result. With access to more services, we're growing used to having fewer skills. This means we hold our few skills at a premium. It is insufficient to be good at many things in a world that always seems to demand each person provide singular greatness in one thing. As a result, we lose sight of just how well-rounded and beautiful worship can be in our own bodies, and in doing so we short change the full Body of Christ.

Worship is the right gift at the right time
I hope this helps. We deeply struggle with perfectionism. I've yet to meet a person who doesn't struggle with perfectionism on some level. For some it's the constant hope of accomplishing their ideal for perfection. For others it is the apathy they wear as a guard against the strain, a defense mechanism to preserve sanity. Yet God calls us to a totally different level of "perfect" than we're thinking of here when we are created for what God deems "good."

Rather than thinking of a "Perfect 10" we should think more of a "perfect fit." There are many things you do that may be the perfect fit for your given situation. When you add God in the mix, and a heart of worship, then fitting into the right spot at the right time becomes much more likely. Our vast creative potential is like puzzle pieces snapping together so that a beautiful image can be formed. From one moment to the next we will find ourselves doing things we haven't perfected, but they may prove to be perfectly fitting in that moment.

You don't have to be a trained counselor to be the right shoulder to cry on. You don't have to be a competition winning vocalist to be the right person to sing a song of hope. You don't have to be an accomplished author to write the story that changes someone's perspective. You don't have to be a super hero to keep someone from making a grave mistake. God can use you where you are and make you perfectly fitting for that moment if your love of God guides your willingness to act.

Fear always seeks to destroy these great moments of worship.

There is a reason why "do not be afraid" is the most repeated phrase in the Bible. Typically it was coupled with news that something uncomfortable was about to be expected of the recipient of the message. God has never been driven by finding the "Perfect 10" candidate for the job. Rather, God's chosen ones are often the *perfectly fitting* ones that, upon the grace-enabled completion of the task, bring about a result which is something the Creator deems as "good."

As you've read this book I hope you've been

reminded of the strengths you have, those creative gifts that you can use greatly for the Kingdom. However, it may very well be some of the underdeveloped gifts you have that most interest the Creator. After all, this is the God who calls a stammering murderer to lead the Children of Israel out of Egypt and to deliver the Law to them. Moses was certainly no silk-tongued negotiator or narrator.

When we accept that we are called to be fully available as conduits of worship, it may mean that parts of us we aren't used to presenting for worship are some of the first called to the task. While this can create a great rush of fear, we must trust that our Creator sees and understands in a way beyond our own understanding.

A prayer for courage
A few years ago, after the time of eviction and depression I mentioned early in this book, I was working a steady job doing home repairs and renovations. The benefits of the job included providing for my wife and daughter, our debt was being lowered at a satisfactory rate, and we were starting to prepare for our next steps. Right in the middle of all of this, the clear direction came that we needed to move back to where the previous failures had occurred so that I could finish my degree and move closer to my lifelong

career in ministry.

While there was some trepidation things quickly began to fall together and I was so *excited*! I shared this with a group of guys I was meeting with regularly for Bible study that were a wonderful accountability group. Not only did I share about how things were starting to come together for our move, but also how I was so thrilled about it all. Just as with all other praises and requests, the next step was to pray.

One of the men was asked to pray, a former missionary and kind-hearted man of God, and he started out with an earnest prayer. Before long the prayer began to focus on courage. "And give Nate courage for what is before him," he prayed. A few seconds later he continued, "Don't let fear take hold, but strengthen and encourage him for what lies ahead." At first I was taken aback by this prayer. Had he missed what I'd just said about how excited I was about this move and how everything was coming together? But then I realized that he had a profound wisdom, and I began to join him in earnestly asking for those things despite how I felt in that moment.

I can't tell you how many times that prayer came to mind as the job I'd secured fell through right as I was moving my family back to the city. It was a constant reminder in scary times. We left the city when we were evicted. We returned to almost immediate homelessness. It should have been devastating. Instead, it wasn't even a time of depression.

Don't get me wrong, things were very difficult and stressful. But as I held on tight to the Creator and kept pressing on, the plan began to unfold. Faithful friends found ways to help provide for us. A job came along that helped satisfy some of my desire for youth ministry even though it wasn't exactly what I'd wanted. Re-enrollment in school was delayed, but it did happen and, a few months later, graduation followed. In the midst of that time, I had to do many things that played to my weaknesses, not my strengths. Yet in allowing that time to be about worship, the Creator was making something "good" that I couldn't manage on my own.

We'll never realize how "good" we can be until we give everything to God, even our fear and shame, so that something more incredible can be put in their place.

Chapter Ten
Shameless Worship

As I think back on all that this book has meant in my own life and all that my eyes have been opened to as I read and prepared to create this work I am shocked by one thing above all else. I wish I could say that what is shocking is just how good God is, or just how amazing being called to create can feel, but I already had a good notion of such things. Rather, what has blown me away is the blatantly irrational fear we have of giving God the glory.

Here—joining us in this journey—is the Creator of the universe. There is some need to admit that God is a pretty important figure throughout time, not to mention the only one to hold time. Yet we get sheepish and quiet about being called to do things. We grow embarrassed and want to escape participating with God in those callings. We allow fear to fill our lives until we're paralyzed or even defiant of God's presence—either staying put when we should go, or running in the opposite direction—because we mute our adoration.

Going with God on this journey is an ongoing act of worship, it is a relationship of adoration, and we never want to withhold our open feelings of love toward God. Withholding such love only hurts others who need to join in this journey, which are desperate for such a love relationship in a world that has so deeply and disturbingly twisted and abused the concept of love. If we're not careful we'll be pushing them away from God's love because we're trying to silence the presence of it in our own lives.

The shame is not from God, there is no shame in God. We started this book talking about the creation account of Genesis chapter one. We need to take a few moments to now address the fall in Genesis chapter three. Adam and Eve go from daily walking with God—actually *walking with God* in the Garden—to trying to cover up their bodies and hiding from God. When we are open to walking with God we do so without shame. When we try to stand equal to God—pushing away the journey of love—then shame overwhelms us. That is the opening for many terrible things to invade our lives. God immediately points out that something is wrong because those who are fully open to walking with God are not ashamed of such a wonderful thing.

Missteps and shameful abandonment
There is one more story with David that I would like to address. In 2 Samuel (chapter 6) David is returning the Ark of the Covenant to its rightful place in Jerusalem. This was a big deal! The Ark

of the Covenant was where God was present. It had been carried during the journeys of the children of Israel through the wilderness and back into the Promised Land. The Ark of the Covenant had circled Jericho. What it represented as it was hoisted on the shoulders of Levite priests was that God was *still* walking with the people of God.

David decides to break the Law about how the Ark of the Covenant is supposed to be transported. Rather than letting the presence of God *walk* with God's chosen people upon the shoulders of the priests David opts to load it up on a cart pulled by oxen. Just like Adam and Eve the journey with God is abandoned for the willingness to try to be as important as God. Unfortunately, as the bumpy cart ride continues the Ark of the Covenant begins to tip and fall and Uzzah, one of David's men, reaches out to balance the Ark and ends up dying. David was angry, David was afraid, in truth David was ashamed. Uzzah's death is on David's hands. No longer willing to walk in proper adoration of God David has now cost one of his men greatly.

When we try to live our lives apart from the open adoration of God – not for show, but that deep love for our Creator and Savior that we cannot contain – we put everyone in peril.

David, in his anger, opts to leave the Ark of the Covenant with Obed-Edom the Gittite. He becomes defiant of the presence of God. It's a rash decision. David is denying worship. Obed-Edom accepts this gift—with an openness to worship and an adoration of the presence of God—and the Ark of the Covenant remains in his house for three months. During this time he and his household are *incredibly blessed*.

Return and shameful worship
Hearing that incredible blessing has come upon the household of Obed-Edom in the three months of having the Ark of the Covenant leads David to return. The Ark is properly restored to its place. David returns with the Ark worshiping and adoring God. Evidently it's quite a party. While we're unclear as to what sort of disarray David's clothing ends up in as he jumps, dances and praises his God it is clear that he is more exposed than it would be believed is appropriate for a king out in public.

One of Saul's daughters sees him and she calls him out on this supposedly atrocious act. However, David is enraptured with worship, points out that what he is doing is being done before the LORD, and that he's willing to be even more undignified, until even he feels humiliated, in worship of God. I'm reminded of Paul's admission in the beginning of Galatians that he isn't looking for the approval of humankind, but the approval of God. There is no more important relationship to have intact than that journey, walking, creating, adoring relationship with God.

At any point shame will be the attack. The adversary to creation and re-creation wants to rob us of our peace and joy to disrupt the journey with God. Nothing is too low to be attempted, too. We may grow too scared to start, we may seek to abandon in the middle, or we complete the task and then refuse to share the miraculous goodness of God journey with us throughout. All of these things are those moments where the adversary has gotten enough hold on us that we're hiding in the trees as God walks the Garden, or leaving the Ark where it doesn't belong because we're angry about our own mistake.

My hope and prayer is that something in this book has sparked the kindling that your flame of passion for God and the creative opportunities set before you will grow. The world serves this adversary, and all too often we let those odds feel insurmountable, but the God who created this world is still doing a restorative work in it and we are called to be creative participants that it may once more be deemed as "good."

God is still calling
God is still calling us—the creative creation—to speak out against the world that mocks the LORD by rightly serving and creating. The world says, "No one cares for the poor, hurting, wounded, marginalized and outsider." Then the image-bearers speak the Word of God into creation by embodying and creating these very things! At this point giants are silenced and lives are changed. The world says, "Believers have no skill, passion, originality, creativity, or passion." Then those embracing that we are created in God's likeness speak the Word of God into creation boldly by participating in that which is "good" and giants are silenced and lives are changed.

What this means is the world waits for your participation, so that giants may fall, and the fuller truth of God's "good" creation may re-emerge.

It's time to join in the journey.

Author Information

Nate Pruitt is an author and speaker out of Nashville, Tennessee. He is also a minister to youth and families and an avid proponent of enabling people to journey with God in their creative callings. A father of three he spends a great portion of his time changing diapers, dispensing meals, and encouraging good choices—all of which are a part of his creative calling at this time.

Made in the USA
Charleston, SC
15 March 2014